all-new Low-Carb COOKBOOK

Recipes to help you lose weight!

Publications International, Ltd.

Favorite Brand Name Recipes at www.fbnr.com

Pictured on the front cover: Roast Chicken with Peppers *(page 46)*.
Pictured on the back cover *(clockwise from top):* Spinach, Cheese and Prosciutto-Stuffed Chicken Breast *(page 36),* Steak with Zesty Merlot Sauce *(page 32)* and Strawberry-Topped Cheesecake Cups *(page 88)*.

ISBN: 1-4127-0257-7

Manufactured in China.

8 7 6 5 4 3 2 1

Nutritional Analysis: The nutritional information that appears with each recipe was submitted in part by the participating companies and associations. Every effort has been made to check the accuracy of these numbers. However, because numerous variables account for a wide range of values for certain foods, nutritive analyses in this book should be considered approximate.

Microwave Cooking: Microwave ovens vary in wattage. Use the cooking times as guidelines and check for doneness before adding more time.

Preparation/Cooking Times: Preparation times are based on the approximate amount of time required to assemble the recipe before cooking, baking, chilling or serving. These times include preparation steps such as measuring, chopping and mixing. The fact that some preparations and cooking can be done simultaneously is taken into account. Preparation of optional ingredients and serving suggestions is not included.

Note: Neither Publications International, Ltd., nor the authors, editors or publisher take responsibility for any possible consequences from any treatment, procedure, exercise, dietary modification, action, or applications of medication or preparation by any person reading or following the information in this cookbook. The publication of this book does not constitute the practice of medicine, and this cookbook does not attempt to replace your physician or your pharmacist. **Before undertaking any course of treatment, the authors, editors and publisher advise the reader to check with a physician or other health care provider.**

contents

PAGE 20

PAGE 50

PAGE 60

eye
openers

SWISS CANADIAN BACON AND EGGS

MAKES 4 SERVINGS

　8 eggs
¼ cup milk
½ teaspoon salt
¼ teaspoon black pepper
⅓ cup finely chopped green onions, divided
　Nonstick cooking spray
4 slices Canadian bacon, cut in half
1 cup (4 ounces) shredded Swiss cheese

1. Preheat broiler.

2. Whisk together eggs, milk, salt and pepper in medium bowl until well blended. Stir in all but 2 tablespoons onions.

3. Spray 12-inch ovenproof skillet with cooking spray; heat over medium-low heat until hot. Add egg mixture. Cover and cook 14 minutes or until almost set.

4. Arrange bacon in pinwheel on top of egg mixture. Sprinkle with cheese; broil 2 minutes or until cheese is bubbly. Top with remaining 2 tablespoons onion. Cut into 4 wedges. Serve immediately.

NUTRIENTS PER SERVING			
Calories	**309**	Cholesterol	**466mg**
Total fat	**20g**	Sodium	**898mg**
Protein	**27g**	Fiber	**<1g**
Carbohydrate	**4g**		

SWISS CANADIAN BACON AND EGGS

BLUEBERRY CHEESECAKE MUFFINS

MAKES 12 SERVINGS

8 ounces cream cheese, softened
1 cup plus 1 tablespoon no-calorie sugar substitute for baking, divided
2 eggs
1 teaspoon grated lemon peel
1 teaspoon vanilla
¾ cup bran flakes cereal
½ cup all-purpose flour
½ cup soy flour
2 teaspoons baking powder
¼ teaspoon salt
¾ cup milk
3 tablespoons melted butter
4 tablespoons no-sugar-added blueberry fruit spread
½ teaspoon ground cinnamon

1. Preheat oven to 350°F. Spray 12 muffin cups with nonstick cooking spray.

2. Beat cream cheese in medium bowl on high speed of electric mixer until smooth. Beat in ¾ cup sugar substitute, 1 egg, lemon peel and vanilla.

3. Stir together cereal, flours, ¼ cup sugar substitute, baking powder and salt in medium bowl. In separate small bowl, whisk milk, butter and 1 egg until blended; pour over cereal mixture. Mix gently just until blended.

4. Spoon about 2 tablespoons batter into each muffin cup. Spread 1 teaspoon fruit spread over batter. Spread cream cheese mixture over fruit spread. Combine remaining 1 tablespoon sugar substitute and cinnamon; sprinkle mixture evenly over cream cheese mixture.

5. Bake 30 to 35 minutes or until toothpick inserted into centers comes out clean. Cool muffins 10 minutes in pan on wire rack. Remove muffins from pan and cool. Serve warm or at room temperature. Refrigerate leftover muffins.

NUTRIENTS PER SERVING			
Calories	178	Cholesterol	66mg
Total fat	11g	Sodium	255mg
Protein	5g	Fiber	1g
Carbohydrate	14g		

BLUEBERRY CHEESECAKE MUFFINS

eye openers

CHEDDARY SAUSAGE FRITTATA
MAKES 4 SERVINGS

4 eggs
¼ cup milk
1 package (12 ounces) bulk breakfast pork sausage
1 poblano pepper,* seeded and chopped
1 cup (4 ounces) shredded Cheddar cheese

*Poblano peppers can sting and irritate the skin; wear rubber gloves when handling peppers and do not touch eyes. Wash hands after handling.

1. Preheat broiler.

2. Combine eggs and milk in medium bowl; whisk until well blended. Set aside.

3. Heat 12-inch ovenproof nonstick skillet over medium-high heat until hot. Add sausage; cook and stir 4 minutes or until no longer pink, breaking up sausage with spoon. Drain sausage on paper towels; set aside.

4. Add chopped poblano to same skillet; cook and stir 2 minutes or until crisp-tender. Return sausage to skillet with egg mixture; stir until blended. Cover and cook 10 minutes on medium-low or until eggs are almost set.

5. Sprinkle cheese over egg mixture; broil 2 minutes or until cheese is melted. Cut into 4 wedges. Serve immediately.

Tip: If skillet is not ovenproof, wrap the handle in heavy-duty foil before broiling frittata.

NUTRIENTS PER SERVING			
Calories	**498**	Cholesterol	**292mg**
Total fat	**39g**	Sodium	**673mg**
Protein	**24g**	Fiber	**<1g**
Carbohydrate	**5g**		

CHEDDARY SAUSAGE FRITTATA

DEEP SOUTH HAM AND REDEYE GRAVY

MAKES 4 SERVINGS

1 tablespoon butter
1 ham steak (about 1⅓ pounds)
1 cup strong coffee
¾ teaspoon sugar
¼ teaspoon hot pepper sauce

1. Heat large skillet over medium-high heat until hot. Add butter; tilt skillet to coat bottom. Add ham steak; cook 3 minutes. Turn; cook 2 minutes longer or until lightly browned. Remove ham to serving platter; set aside and keep warm.

2. Add coffee, sugar and pepper sauce to same skillet. Bring to a boil over high heat; boil 2 to 3 minutes or until liquid is reduced to ¼ cup liquid, scraping up any brown bits. Serve gravy over ham.

Serving Suggestion: Serve ham steak with sautéed greens and poached eggs.

NUTRIENTS PER SERVING			
Calories	**215**	Cholesterol	**76mg**
Total fat	**9g**	Sodium	**2mg**
Protein	**30g**	Fiber	**0g**
Carbohydrate	**1g**		

DEEP SOUTH HAM AND REDEYE GRAVY

FABULOUS FETA FRITTATA

MAKES 4 SERVINGS

2 tablespoons butter or olive oil
8 eggs
¼ cup whipping cream or half-and-half
¼ cup chopped fresh basil
½ teaspoon salt
¼ teaspoon freshly ground black pepper
1 package (4 ounces) crumbled feta cheese with basil, olives and sun-dried tomatoes *or* 1 cup crumbled feta cheese
¼ cup pine nuts

1. Preheat broiler. Melt butter in 10-inch ovenproof skillet with sloped sides over medium heat. Tilt skillet so bottom and sides are well coated with butter. Beat eggs. Add cream, basil, salt and pepper; mix well. Pour mixture into skillet. Cover; cook 8 to 10 minutes or until eggs are set around edges (center will be wet).

2. Sprinkle cheese and pine nuts evenly over frittata. Transfer to broiler; broil 4 to 5 inches from heat source for 2 minutes or until center of frittata is set and pine nuts are golden brown. Cut into wedges.

Tip: If skillet is not ovenproof, wrap the handle in heavy-duty foil before broiling frittata.

NUTRIENTS PER SERVING			
Calories	**378**	Cholesterol	**487mg**
Total fat	**32g**	Sodium	**797mg**
Protein	**19g**	Fiber	**<1g**
Carbohydrate	**4g**		

FABULOUS FETA FRITTATA

CHEESE BLINTZES WITH STRAWBERRIES & SOUR CREAM

MAKES 4 SERVINGS

3 tablespoons melted butter, divided
1 container (15 ounces) whole-milk ricotta cheese
1 tablespoon plus 2 teaspoons granulated sugar substitute, divided
1 teaspoon vanilla
⅛ teaspoon ground nutmeg
8 (8-inch) prepared crêpes
½ cup sliced fresh strawberries
¼ cup sour cream

1. Preheat oven to 350°F. Brush 1 tablespoon butter over bottom of 13×9-inch baking dish.

2. Combine cheese, 1 tablespoon sugar substitute, vanilla and nutmeg in food processor; process until smooth. Spoon scant ¼ cup mixture onto center of each crêpe. Fold outside edges of crêpe over filling; roll up from bottom. Place crêpes, seam side down, in prepared dish. Brush remaining 2 tablespoons butter over crêpes. Bake uncovered 18 to 20 minutes or until hot.

3. Meanwhile, combine strawberries and remaining 2 teaspoons sugar substitute; set aside at room temperature. Transfer crêpes to serving plates; top with strawberries. Serve with sour cream.

Tip: Look for shelf-stable packages of crêpes near the berries in the supermarket produce section.

NUTRIENTS PER SERVING			
Calories	**362**	Cholesterol	**94mg**
Total fat	**27g**	Sodium	**289mg**
Protein	**15g**	Fiber	**<1g**
Carbohydrate	**16g**		

CHEESE BLINTZES WITH STRAWBERRIES & SOUR CREAM

lunch options

CHUNKY CHICKEN AND VEGETABLE SOUP

MAKES 4 SERVINGS

1 tablespoon vegetable oil
1 boneless skinless chicken breast (4 ounces), diced
½ cup chopped green bell pepper
½ cup thinly sliced celery
2 green onions, sliced
2 cans (14½ ounces each) chicken broth
1 cup water
½ cup sliced carrots
2 tablespoons cream
1 tablespoon finely chopped parsley
¼ teaspoon dried thyme leaves
⅛ teaspoon black pepper

1. Heat oil in large saucepan over medium heat. Add chicken; cook and stir 4 to 5 minutes or until no longer pink. Add bell pepper, celery and onions. Cook and stir 7 minutes or until vegetables are tender.

2. Add broth, water, carrots, cream, parsley, thyme and black pepper. Simmer 10 minutes or until carrots are tender.

NUTRIENTS PER SERVING			
Calories	**130**	Cholesterol	**27mg**
Total fat	**8g**	Sodium	**895mg**
Protein	**9g**	Fiber	**1g**
Carbohydrate	**5g**		

CHUNKY CHICKEN AND VEGETABLE SOUP

SOUTHWESTERN OMELET WRAP

MAKES 1 SERVING

2 teaspoons cornstarch
1 tablespoon water
1 egg
Nonstick cooking spray
3 tablespoons canned refried beans, warmed
1 tablespoon bacon bits
¼ cup (1 ounce) shredded Monterey Jack or Cheddar cheese
2 tablespoons chunky salsa
½ cup finely shredded romaine or iceberg lettuce

1. To make omelet, dissolve cornstarch in water in small bowl. Add egg; whisk until blended.

2. Spray large nonstick skillet lightly with cooking spray; heat over medium-high heat. Add egg mixture, tilting skillet to cover bottom of skillet. Cook 1 to 2 minutes or until set. Turn omelet over; cook 30 seconds. Turn out onto cutting board, browned side down.

3. To make wrap, spread beans to edge of omelet. Sprinkle evenly with bacon bits, cheese, salsa and lettuce.

4. Gently roll up, sealing with refried beans. Serve immediately; or, wrap in plastic wrap and refrigerate.

NUTRIENTS PER SERVING			
Calories	**286**	Cholesterol	**243mg**
Total fat	**17g**	Sodium	**796mg**
Protein	**19g**	Fiber	**4g**
Carbohydrate	**16g**		

SOUTHWESTERN OMELET WRAP

PEPPERONI PIZZA SOUP

MAKES 4 SERVINGS

1 tablespoon oil
1 cup sliced mushrooms
1 cup chopped green bell pepper
½ cup chopped onion
1 can (15 ounces) pizza sauce
1 can (14½ ounces) chicken broth
1 cup water
3 ounces sliced pepperoni
1 teaspoon dried oregano
1 cup (4 ounces) shredded mozzarella cheese

1. Heat oil in large saucepan over medium heat. Add mushrooms, bell pepper and onion. Cook, stirring frequently, 7 minutes or until vegetables are tender.

2. Stir in pizza sauce, broth, water, pepperoni and oregano. Bring to a boil. Reduce heat and heat simmer 5 minutes. Top with cheese just before serving.

Tip: People following low-carb meal plans often say they miss pizza more than any other food. This recipe satisfies that craving with great pizza flavor and a minimum carbohydrate count!

NUTRIENTS PER SERVING			
Calories	**296**	Cholesterol	**32mg**
Total fat	**21g**	Sodium	**1mg**
Protein	**15g**	Fiber	**3g**
Carbohydrate	**14g**		

PEPPERONI PIZZA SOUP

NO-KNEAD SANDWICH BREAD

MAKES 30 (1/4-INCH) SLICES

2 packages (2¼ teaspoons) active dry yeast
¾ cup warm water (110° to 115°F)
3 tablespoons canola oil
1 cup all-purpose flour
⅔ cup uncooked old-fashioned oats
¼ cup soy flour*
¼ cup wheat gluten*
¼ cup sesame seeds*
2 teaspoons sugar substitute
1 teaspoon salt

Soy flour, wheat gluten and sesame seeds are available in the natural foods sections of many supermarkets and at health food stores.

1. Stir yeast into water in small bowl; let stand 5 minutes. Add oil.

2. Combine all-purpose flour, oats, soy flour, gluten, sesame seeds, sugar substitute and salt in food processor fitted with plastic dough blade. Using on/off pulsing action, process until blended.

3. With processor running, slowly pour yeast mixture through feed tube; then using on/off pulsing action, process until dough comes together and forms a mass. Unlock processor lid, but do not remove; let dough rise 1 hour or until doubled in bulk.

4. Spray 8×4×2-inch loaf pan with nonstick cooking spray. Using on/off pulsing action, process briefly until dough comes together and forms a ball. Turn dough onto floured work surface. Shape into disc. (Dough will be slightly sticky.) Roll dough on floured surface into 12×8-inch rectangle. Roll up from short side; fold under ends and place in prepared pan. Cover with towel; let rise in warm place 45 minutes or until doubled in bulk.

5. Preheat oven to 375°F. Bake 35 minutes or until bread is golden brown and sounds hollow when tapped. Remove from pan and cool completely on wire rack. Cut into ¼-inch slices with serrated knife.

NUTRIENTS PER SERVING			
Calories	**51**	Cholesterol	**0mg**
Total fat	**2g**	Sodium	**79mg**
Protein	**2g**	Fiber	**1g**
Carbohydrate	**6g**		

TWO-MINUTE TUNA SALAD SANDWICH
MAKES 3 SERVINGS

1 6-ounce can water-packed solid albacore tuna, drained and flaked
½ cup celery slices
2 tablespoons plus 1½ teaspoons mayonnaise or reduced-fat mayonnaise (not nonfat)
1 tablespoon drained capers
½ teaspoon onion powder
6 ¼-inch-thick slices No-Knead Sandwich Bread (page 24)
Lettuce leaves

1. Combine all ingredients except bread and lettuce in small bowl; mix well.

2. Spread ⅓ tuna mixture on each of 3 bread slices. Top with lettuce leaves and remaining bread slices.

NUTRIENTS PER SERVING			
Calories	**261**	Cholesterol	**31mg**
Total fat	**15g**	Sodium	**560mg**
Protein	**18g**	Fiber	**2g**
Carbohydrate	**12g**		

NO-KNEAD SANDWICH BREAD

VEGETABLE STRATA

MAKES 6 SERVINGS

    2 slices white bread, cubed
¼ cup shredded reduced-fat Swiss cheese
½ cup sliced carrots
½ cup sliced mushrooms
¼ cup chopped onion
    1 clove garlic, crushed
    1 teaspoon FLEISCHMANN'S® Original Margarine
½ cup chopped tomato
½ cup snow peas
    1 cup EGG BEATERS® Healthy Real Egg Product
¾ cup skim milk

Place bread cubes evenly on bottom of greased 1½-quart casserole dish. Sprinkle with cheese; set aside.

In medium nonstick skillet, over medium heat, sauté carrots, mushrooms, onion and garlic in margarine until tender. Stir in tomato and snow peas; cook 1 to 2 minutes more. Spoon over cheese. In small bowl, combine Egg Beaters® and milk; pour over vegetable mixture. Bake at 375°F for 45 to 50 minutes or until knife inserted in center comes out clean. Let stand 10 minutes before serving.

Prep Time: 15 minutes
Cook Time: 55 minutes

NUTRIENTS PER SERVING			
Calories	**83**	Cholesterol	**3mg**
Total fat	**1g**	Sodium	**161mg**
Protein	**8g**	Fiber	**1g**
Carbohydrate	**10g**		

VEGETABLE STRATA

CIOPPINO

MAKES 4 SERVINGS

1 teaspoon olive oil
1 large onion, chopped
1 cup sliced celery, with celery tops
1 clove garlic, minced
4 cups water
1 fish-flavor bouillon cube
1 tablespoon salt-free Italian herb seasoning
¼ pound cod or other boneless mild-flavored fish fillets
1 large tomato, chopped
1 can (10 ounces) baby clams, rinsed and drained (optional)
¼ pound uncooked small shrimp, peeled and deveined
¼ pound uncooked bay scallops
¼ cup flaked crabmeat or crabmeat blend
2 tablespoons fresh lemon juice

1. Heat olive oil in large saucepan over medium heat until hot. Add onion, celery and garlic. Cook and stir 5 minutes or until onion is soft. Add water, bouillon cube and Italian seasoning. Cover and bring to a boil over high heat.

2. Cut cod fillets into ½-inch pieces. Add cod and tomato to saucepan. Reduce heat to medium-low; simmer 10 to 15 minutes or until seafood is opaque. Add clams, if desired, shrimp, scallops, crabmeat and lemon juice. Heat through. Garnish with lemon wedges, if desired.

Prep and Cook Time: 30 minutes

NUTRIENTS PER SERVING			
Calories	122	Cholesterol	75mg
Total fat	2g	Sodium	412mg
Protein	18g	Fiber	2g
Carbohydrate	8g		

CIOPPINO

QUICK ORANGE CHICKEN

MAKES 4 SERVINGS

2 tablespoons frozen orange juice concentrate
1 tablespoon no-sugar-added orange marmalade
1 teaspoon Dijon mustard
¼ teaspoon salt
4 boneless skinless chicken breasts (about 1 pound)
½ cup fresh orange sections
2 tablespoons chopped fresh parsley

Microwave Directions

1. For sauce, combine juice concentrate, marmalade, mustard and salt in 8-inch shallow round microwavable dish until juice concentrate is thawed.

2. Add chicken, coating both sides with sauce. Arrange chicken around edge of dish without overlapping. Cover with vented plastic wrap. Microwave at HIGH (100%) 3 minutes; turn chicken over. Microwave at MEDIUM-HIGH (70%) 4 minutes, or until chicken is no longer pink in center.

3. Remove chicken to serving plate. Microwave remaining sauce at HIGH (100%) 2 to 3 minutes or until slightly thickened.

4. To serve, spoon sauce over chicken; top with orange sections and parsley.

NUTRIENTS PER SERVING			
Calories	**157**	Cholesterol	**60mg**
Total fat	**3g**	Sodium	**207mg**
Protein	**23g**	Fiber	**1g**
Carbohydrate	**10g**		

QUICK ORANGE CHICKEN

savvy suppers

STEAK WITH ZESTY MERLOT SAUCE

MAKES 4 SERVINGS

½ cup merlot wine
2 tablespoons Worcestershire sauce
1 tablespoon balsamic vinegar
1 teaspoon sugar
1 teaspoon beef bouillon granules
½ teaspoon dried thyme leaves
2 beef ribeye steaks (8 ounces each)
2 tablespoons finely chopped parsley

1. Combine wine, Worcestershire sauce, vinegar, sugar, bouillon granules and thyme; set aside.

2. Heat large nonstick skillet over high heat until hot. Add steaks; cook 3 minutes on each side. Turn steaks again and cook 3 to 6 minutes longer over medium heat or until desired doneness.

3. Cut steaks in half; arrange on serving platter. Place in oven to keep warm.

4. Add wine mixture to same skillet. Bring to a boil; cook and stir 1 minute, scraping up any brown bits. Spoon over steaks. Sprinkle with parsley; serve immediately.

NUTRIENTS PER SERVING			
Calories	287	Cholesterol	58mg
Total fat	17g	Sodium	294mg
Protein	23g	Fiber	<1g
Carbohydrate	4g		

STEAKS WITH ZESTY MERLOT SAUCE

SZECHWAN SEAFOOD STIR-FRY

MAKES 4 SERVINGS

1 package (10 ounces) fresh spinach leaves
4 teaspoons dark sesame oil, divided
4 cloves garlic, minced and divided
¼ cup reduced-sodium soy sauce
1 tablespoon cornstarch
1 tablespoon dry sherry or sake
1 medium red bell pepper, cut into thin, 1-inch-long strips
1½ teaspoons minced fresh or bottled ginger root
¾ pound peeled, deveined large shrimp, thawed if frozen
½ pound fresh bay scallops
2 teaspoons sesame seeds, toasted

1. Rinse spinach in cold water; drain. Heat 2 teaspoons oil in large saucepan over medium heat. Add 2 cloves garlic; stir-fry 1 minute. Add spinach; cover and steam 4 to 5 minutes or until spinach is wilted, turning with tongs after 3 minutes. Remove from heat; keep covered.

2. Meanwhile, combine soy sauce, cornstarch and sherry until smooth; set aside. Heat remaining 2 teaspoons oil in large nonstick skillet over medium-high heat. Add bell pepper; stir-fry 2 minutes. Add remaining 2 cloves garlic and ginger; stir-fry 1 minute. Add shrimp; stir-fry 2 minutes. Add scallops; stir-fry 1 minute or until shrimp and scallops are opaque. Add soy sauce mixture; stir-fry 1 minute or until sauce thickens.

3. Stir spinach mixture and transfer to 4 individual plates; top with seafood mixture and sesame seeds.

Tip: Substitute one large head bok choy, thinly sliced, for spinach. Increase steaming time to 8 minutes or until bok choy is tender.

NUTRIENTS PER SERVING			
Calories	**249**	Cholesterol	**147mg**
Total fat	**9g**	Sodium	**960mg**
Protein	**31g**	Fiber	**7g**
Carbohydrate	**10g**		

SZECHWAN SEAFOOD STIR-FRY

SPINACH, CHEESE AND PROSCIUTTO-STUFFED CHICKEN BREASTS

MAKES 4 SERVINGS

4 boneless skinless chicken breasts (about 4 ounces each)
Salt and black pepper
4 slices (½ ounce each) prosciutto*
4 slices (½ ounce each) smoked provolone
1 cup spinach leaves, chopped
4 tablespoons all-purpose flour, divided
1 tablespoon olive oil
1 tablespoon butter
1 cup chicken broth
1 tablespoon heavy cream

Prosciutto, an Italian ham, is seasoned, cured and air-dried, not smoked. Look for imported or domestic prosciutto in delis and Italian food markets.

1. Preheat oven to 350°F.

2. To form pocket, cut each chicken breast horizontally almost to the opposite edge. Fold back top half of breast; sprinkle lightly with salt and pepper. Place 1 slice prosciutto, 1 slice provolone and ¼ cup spinach on each chicken breast. Fold top half of breasts over filling.

3. Spread 3 tablespoons flour on plate. Holding chicken breast closed, coat in flour; shake off excess. Lightly sprinkle chicken with salt and pepper.

4. Heat oil and butter in large skillet over medium heat. Place chicken in skillet; cook about 4 minutes on each side or until browned.

5. Transfer chicken to shallow baking dish. Bake in oven 10 minutes or until chicken is no longer pink and juices run clear.

6. Whisk chicken broth and cream into remaining 1 tablespoon flour in small bowl. Pour chicken broth mixture into same skillet; heat over medium heat, stirring constantly, until sauce thickens, about 3 minutes. Spoon sauce onto serving plates; top with chicken breasts.

Tip: Swiss, Gruyére or mozzarella cheese may be substituted for smoked provolone. Thinly sliced deli ham may be substituted for prosciutto.

NUTRIENTS PER SERVING			
Calories	**371**	Cholesterol	**105mg**
Total fat	**23g**	Sodium	**854mg**
Protein	**33g**	Fiber	**<1g**
Carbohydrate	**7g**		

SPINACH, CHEESE AND PROSCIUTTO-STUFFED CHICKEN BREAST

ROAST CHICKEN WITH PEPPERS

MAKES 6 SERVINGS

1 chicken (3 to 3½ pounds), cut into pieces
3 tablespoons olive oil, divided
1½ tablespoons chopped fresh rosemary *or* 1½ teaspoons dried rosemary, crushed
1 tablespoon fresh lemon juice
1¼ teaspoons salt, divided
¾ teaspoon freshly ground black pepper, divided
3 bell peppers (preferably 1 red, 1 yellow and 1 green)
1 medium onion

1. Preheat oven to 375°F. Rinse chicken in cold water; pat dry with paper towels. Place in shallow roasting pan.

2. Combine 2 tablespoons oil, rosemary and lemon juice; brush over chicken. Sprinkle 1 teaspoon salt and ½ teaspoon pepper over chicken. Roast 15 minutes.

3. Cut bell peppers lengthwise into ½-inch-thick strips. Slice onion into thin wedges. Toss vegetables with remaining 1 tablespoon oil, ¼ teaspoon salt and ¼ teaspoon pepper. Spoon vegetables around chicken; roast until vegetables are tender and chicken is no longer pink in center, about 40 minutes. Serve chicken with vegetables and pan juices.

NUTRIENTS PER SERVING			
Calories	**428**	Cholesterol	**118mg**
Total fat	**32g**	Sodium	**575mg**
Protein	**29g**	Fiber	**2g**
Carbohydrate	**6g**		

ROAST CHICKEN WITH PEPPERS

PORK CURRY OVER CAULIFLOWER COUSCOUS

MAKES 6 SERVINGS

3 tablespoons olive oil, divided
2 tablespoons mild curry powder
2 teaspoons prepared crushed garlic
1½ pounds pork (boneless shoulder, loin or chops), cubed
1 red or green bell pepper, seeded and diced
1 tablespoon cider vinegar
½ teaspoon salt
2 cups water
1 large head cauliflower

1. Heat 2 tablespoons oil over medium heat in large saucepan. Add curry powder and garlic; cook and stir 1 to 2 minutes or until garlic is golden.

2. Add pork; stir to coat completely with curry and garlic. Cook and stir 5 to 7 minutes or until pork cubes are barely pink in center. Add bell pepper and vinegar; cook and stir 3 minutes or until bell pepper is soft. Sprinkle with salt.

3. Add water; bring to a boil. Reduce heat and simmer 30 to 45 minutes, stirring occasionally, until liquid is reduced and pork is tender, adding additional water as needed.

4. Meanwhile, trim and core cauliflower; cut into equal pieces. Place in food processor fitted with metal blade. Process using on/off pulsing action until cauliflower is in small uniform pieces about the size of cooked couscous. *Do not purée.*

5. Heat remaining 1 tablespoon oil over medium heat in 12-inch nonstick skillet. Add cauliflower; cook and stir 5 minutes or until cooked crisp-tender. *Do not overcook.* Serve pork curry over cauliflower.

NUTRIENTS PER SERVING			
Calories	267	Cholesterol	69mg
Total fat	15g	Sodium	308mg
Protein	28g	Fiber	5g
Carbohydrate	7g		

PORK CURRY OVER CAULIFLOWER COUSCOUS

BLUE CHEESE-STUFFED SIRLOIN PATTIES

MAKES 4 SERVINGS

1½ **pounds ground beef sirloin**
½ **cup (2 ounces) shredded sharp Cheddar cheese**
¼ **cup crumbled blue cheese**
¼ **cup finely chopped parsley**
2 **teaspoons Dijon mustard**
1 **teaspoon Worcestershire sauce**
1 **clove garlic, minced**
¼ **teaspoon salt**
2 **teaspoons olive oil**
1 **medium red bell pepper, cut into thin strips**

1. Shape beef into 8 patties, about 4 inches in diameter and ¼ inch thick.

2. Combine cheeses, parsley, mustard, Worcestershire sauce, garlic and salt in small bowl; toss gently to blend.

3. Mound ¼ of cheese mixture on each of 4 patties (about 3 tablespoons per patty). Top with remaining 4 patties; pinch edges of patties to seal completely. Set aside.

4. Heat oil in 12-inch nonstick skillet over medium-high heat until hot. Add pepper strips; cook and stir until edges begin to brown. Sprinkle with salt. Remove from skillet and keep warm.

5. Add beef patties to same skillet; cook on medium-high 5 minutes. Turn patties; top with peppers. Cook 4 minutes or until patties are no longer pink in centers (160°F).

NUTRIENTS PER SERVING			
Calories	**463**	Cholesterol	**131mg**
Total fat	**32g**	Sodium	**548mg**
Protein	**38g**	Fiber	**1g**
Carbohydrate	**3g**		

BLUE CHEESE-STUFFED SIRLOIN PATTY

GRILLED RED SNAPPER WITH AVOCADO-PAPAYA SALSA

MAKES 4 SERVINGS

1 teaspoon ground coriander
1 teaspoon paprika
¾ teaspoon salt
⅛ to ¼ teaspoon ground red pepper
1 tablespoon olive oil
4 skinless red snapper or halibut fish fillets (5 to 7 ounces each)
½ cup diced ripe avocado
½ cup diced ripe papaya
2 tablespoons chopped cilantro
1 tablespoon fresh lime juice
4 lime wedges

1. Prepare grill for direct grilling. Combine coriander, paprika, salt and red pepper in small bowl or cup; mix well.

2. Brush oil over fish. Sprinkle 2½ teaspoons spice mixture over fish fillets; set aside remaining spice mixture. Place fish skin side down on oiled grid over medium-hot heat. Grill 5 minutes per side or until fish is opaque.

3. Meanwhile, combine avocado, papaya, cilantro, lime juice and reserved spice mixture in medium bowl; mix well. Serve fish with salsa and garnish with lime wedges

NUTRIENTS PER SERVING			
Calories	**221**	Cholesterol	**51mg**
Total fat	**9g**	Sodium	**559mg**
Protein	**30g**	Fiber	**2g**
Carbohydrate	**5g**		

GRILLED RED SNAPPER WITH AVOCADO-PAPAYA SALSA

BOLOGNESE-STYLE PORK RAGÙ OVER SPAGHETTI SQUASH

MAKES 8 SERVINGS

1½ pounds ground pork
1 cup finely chopped celery
½ cup chopped onion
1 teaspoon prepared crushed garlic *or* 2 cloves garlic, minced
2 tablespoons tomato paste
1 teaspoon Italian seasoning
1 can (14½ ounces) low-sodium chicken broth
½ cup half-and-half
1 spaghetti squash (3 to 4 pounds)
½ cup grated Parmesan (optional)

1. Brown pork in 3-quart saucepan over medium-high heat, stirring to break up meat. Add celery and onion; cook and stir 5 minutes over medium heat or until vegetables are tender. Add garlic, cook and stir 1 minute. Stir in tomato paste and Italian seasoning.

2. Stir in broth. Reduce heat. Simmer 10 to 15 minutes, stirring occasionally.

3. Add half-and-half; cook, stirring constantly, until hot. Skim off excess fat.

4. Meanwhile, pierce spaghetti squash several times with knife. Microwave at HIGH (100%) 15 minutes until squash is tender (squash will yield when pressed with finger). Let cool 10 to 15 minutes. Cut in half, scoop out and discard seeds. Separate flesh into strands with fork; keep squash warm.

5. Serve ½ cup meat sauce over 1 cup spaghetti squash. Sprinkle with 1 tablespoon grated Parmesan, if desired.

Tip: Sauce can be cooked the day before and refrigerated so that chilled fat can be removed and discarded before reheating.

NUTRIENTS PER SERVING			
Calories	333	Cholesterol	75mg
Total fat	22g	Sodium	275mg
Protein	20g	Fiber	2g
Carbohydrate	15g		

BOLOGNESE-STYLE PORK RAGÙ OVER SPAGHETTI SQUASH

slender sides

STIR-FRIED ASPARAGUS

MAKES 6 SERVINGS

½ **pound asparagus**
1 **tablespoon olive or canola oil**
1 **cup celery slices**
½ **cup bottled roasted red peppers, drained and diced**
¼ **teaspoon black pepper**
¼ **cup sliced almonds, toasted***

To toast almonds, place in small dry skillet. Cook over medium heat, stirring constantly, until almonds are lightly browned.

1. Trim ends from asparagus; cut stalks diagonally into 1-inch pieces.

2. Heat oil in 12-inch nonstick skillet over medium-high heat. Add celery; stir fry 2 minutes. Add asparagus and red peppers. Stir-fry 3 to 4 minutes or until asparagus is crisp tender.

3. Add black pepper and almonds; mix until blended.

NUTRIENTS PER SERVING			
Calories	**67**	Cholesterol	**0mg**
Total fat	**5g**	Sodium	**18mg**
Protein	**2g**	Fiber	**2g**
Carbohydrate	**4g**		

STIR-FRIED ASPARAGUS

JALAPEÑO WILD RICE CAKES

MAKES 8 SERVINGS

⅓ **cup wild rice**
¾ **cup water**
½ **teaspoon salt, divided**
1 **tablespoon all-purpose flour**
½ **teaspoon baking powder**
1 **egg**
1 **jalapeño pepper,* finely chopped**
2 **tablespoons minced onion**
1 **tablespoon freshly grated ginger** *or* **2 teaspoons ground ginger**
2 **tablespoons vegetable or olive oil**

*Jalapeño peppers can sting and irritate the skin; wear rubber gloves when handling peppers and do not touch eyes. Wash hands after handling.

1. Combine rice, water and ¼ teaspoon salt in medium saucepan. Bring to a boil. Reduce heat; cover and simmer 40 to 45 minutes or until rice is tender. Drain rice, if necessary; place in medium bowl. Add flour, baking powder and remaining ¼ teaspoon salt; mix until blended.

2. Whisk egg, jalapeño pepper, onion and ginger together in small bowl. Pour egg mixture over rice; mix until well blended.

3. Heat oil in large nonstick skillet over medium heat. Spoon 2 tablespoons rice mixture into pan and shape into cake. Cook, 4 cakes at a time, 3 minutes on each side or until golden brown. Transfer to paper towels. Serve immediately or refrigerate rice cakes for up to 24 hours.

Tip: To reheat cold rice cakes, preheat oven to 400°F. Place rice cakes in single layer on baking sheet; heat 5 minutes.

NUTRIENTS PER SERVING			
Calories	63	Cholesterol	27mg
Total fat	4g	Sodium	330mg
Protein	2g	Fiber	<1g
Carbohydrate	5g		

JALAPEÑO WILD RICE CAKES

BRAISED ORIENTAL CABBAGE

MAKES 6 SIDE-DISH SERVINGS

½ small head green cabbage (about ½ pound)
1 small head bok choy (about ¾ pound)
½ cup fat-free reduced-sodium chicken broth
2 tablespoons reduced-sodium soy sauce
2 tablespoons rice wine vinegar
1 tablespoon brown sugar
¼ teaspoon red pepper flakes (optional)
1 tablespoon water
1 tablespoon cornstarch

1. Cut cabbage into 1-inch pieces. Cut woody stems from bok choy leaves; slice stems into ½-inch pieces. Cut tops of leaves into ½-inch slices; set aside.

2. Combine cabbage and bok choy stems in large nonstick skillet. Add broth, soy sauce, vinegar, brown sugar and red pepper flakes, if desired.

3. Bring to a boil over high heat. Reduce heat to medium. Cover and simmer 5 minutes or until vegetables are crisp-tender.

4. Blend water into cornstarch in small bowl until smooth. Stir into skillet. Cook and stir 1 minute or until sauce boils and thickens.

5. Stir in reserved bok choy leaves; cook 1 minute.

NUTRIENTS PER SERVING			
Calories	34	Cholesterol	0mg
Total fat	1g	Sodium	170mg
Protein	2g	Fiber	1g
Carbohydrate	6g		

BRAISED ORIENTAL CABBAGE

LEMON AND FENNEL MARINATED VEGETABLES

MAKES 4 SERVINGS

1 cup water
2 medium carrots, cut diagonally into ½-inch-thick slices
1 cup small whole fresh mushrooms
1 small red or green bell pepper, cut into ¾-inch pieces
3 tablespoons lemon juice
1 tablespoon sugar
1 tablespoon olive oil
1 clove garlic, minced
½ teaspoon fennel seeds, crushed
½ teaspoon dried basil leaves, crushed
¼ teaspoon black pepper

Bring water to a boil over high heat in small saucepan. Add carrots. Return to a boil. Reduce heat to medium-low. Cover and simmer about 5 minutes or until carrots are crisp-tender. Drain and cool.

Place carrots, mushrooms and bell pepper in large resealable plastic food storage bag. Combine lemon juice, sugar, oil, garlic, fennel seeds, basil and black pepper in small bowl. Pour over vegetables. Close bag securely; turn to coat. Marinate in refrigerator 8 to 24 hours, turning occasionally.

Drain vegetables; discard marinade. Place vegetables in serving dish. Serve with toothpicks.

NUTRIENTS PER SERVING			
Calories	**47**	Cholesterol	**0mg**
Total fat	**1g**	Sodium	**15mg**
Protein	**1g**	Fiber	**2g**
Carbohydrate	**9g**		

LEMON AND FENNEL MARINATED VEGETABLES

ASPARAGUS WITH SESAME-GINGER SAUCE

MAKES 7 SERVINGS

1 tablespoon **SPLENDA®** Granular
1 tablespoon water
1 tablespoon peanut oil
1 tablespoon rice vinegar
1 tablespoon soy sauce
1 tablespoon tahini* (puréed sesame seeds)
1 teaspoon chopped fresh ginger
½ teaspoon chopped garlic
Pinch crushed red pepper
48 medium asparagus spears, trimmed and peeled

*Look for tahini in the ethnic foods section of your supermarket.

1. In a food processor, combine all ingredients except asparagus and mix until thoroughly blended. Set aside.

2. Fill large skillet half-full of water; cover and bring to a boil. Add asparagus and simmer just until crisp-tender, approximately 4 to 5 minutes. Drain well. (Do not rinse.)

3. Transfer to serving platter. Pour sauce over hot asparagus. Serve warm or at room temperature.

Prep Time: 10 minutes
Cook Time: 5 minutes

NUTRIENTS PER SERVING			
Calories	**59**	Cholesterol	**0mg**
Total fat	**3g**	Sodium	**183mg**
Protein	**3g**	Fiber	**2g**
Carbohydrate	**6g**		

ASPARAGUS WITH SESAME-GINGER SAUCE

super salads

CHICKEN SALAD

MAKES 4 SERVINGS

¼ cup mayonnaise
¼ cup sour cream
1 tablespoon lemon juice
1 teaspoon sugar
1 teaspoon grated lemon peel
1 teaspoon Dijon mustard
½ teaspoon salt
⅛ to ¼ teaspoon white pepper
2 cups diced cooked chicken
1 cup sliced celery
¼ cup sliced green onions
    Lettuce leaves
    Crumbled blue cheese (optional)

1. Combine mayonnaise, sour cream, lemon juice, sugar, lemon peel, mustard, salt and pepper in large bowl.

2. Add chicken, celery and green onions; stir to combine. Cover; refrigerate at least 1 hour to allow flavors to blend.

3. Serve salad on lettuce-lined plate. Sprinkle with blue cheese, if desired.

NUTRIENTS PER SERVING			
Calories	**310**	Cholesterol	**69mg**
Total fat	**23g**	Sodium	**442mg**
Protein	**22g**	Fiber	**1g**
Carbohydrate	**4g**		

CHICKEN SALAD

THAI BROCCOLI SALAD

MAKES 4 SERVINGS

¼ cup creamy or chunky peanut butter
2 tablespoons **EQUAL® SPOONFUL***
1½ tablespoons hot water
1 tablespoon lime juice
1 tablespoon light soy sauce
1½ teaspoons dark sesame oil
¼ teaspoon red pepper flakes
2 tablespoons vegetable oil
3 cups fresh broccoli florets
½ cup chopped red bell pepper
¼ cup sliced green onions
1 clove garlic, crushed

*May substitute 3 packets Equal® sweetener.

• Combine peanut butter, Equal®, hot water, lime juice, soy sauce, sesame oil and red pepper flakes until well blended; set aside.

• Heat vegetable oil in large skillet over medium-high heat. Add broccoli, red pepper, green onions and garlic. Stir-fry 3 to 4 minutes until vegetables are tender-crisp. Remove from heat and stir in peanut butter mixture.

• Serve warm or at room temperature.

NUTRIENTS PER SERVING			
Calories	**199**	Cholesterol	**0mg**
Total fat	**17g**	Sodium	**342mg**
Protein	**6g**	Fiber	**4g**
Carbohydrate	**9g**		

THAI BROCCOLI SALAD

RASPBERRY MANGO SALAD

MAKES 4 SERVINGS

2 cups arugula
1 cup torn Bibb or Boston lettuce
½ cup watercress, stems removed
1 cup diced mango
¾ cup fresh raspberries
¼ cup (1½ ounces) crumbled blue cheese
1 tablespoon olive oil
1 tablespoon water
1 tablespoon raspberry vinegar
⅛ teaspoon salt
⅛ teaspoon black pepper

1. Combine arugula, lettuce, watercress, mango, raspberries and cheese in medium bowl.

2. Shake remaining ingredients in small jar. Pour over salad; toss to coat. Serve immediately.

NUTRIENTS PER SERVING			
Calories	**98**	Cholesterol	**8mg**
Total fat	**8g**	Sodium	**227mg**
Protein	**3g**	Fiber	**2g**
Carbohydrate	**4g**		

RASPBERRY MANGO SALAD

GREENS AND BROCCOLI SALAD WITH PEPPY VINAIGRETTE

MAKES 4 SERVINGS

4 sun-dried tomato halves (not packed in oil)
3 cups torn washed red-tipped or plain leaf lettuce
1½ cups broccoli florets
1 cup sliced fresh mushrooms
⅓ cup sliced radishes
2 tablespoons water
1 tablespoon balsamic vinegar
1 teaspoon vegetable oil
¼ teaspoon chicken bouillon granules
¼ teaspoon dried chervil leaves
¼ teaspoon dry mustard
⅛ teaspoon ground red pepper

1. Pour enough boiling water over tomatoes in small bowl to cover. Let stand 5 minutes; drain. Chop tomatoes. Combine tomatoes, lettuce, broccoli, mushrooms and radishes in large salad bowl.

2. Combine 2 tablespoons water, vinegar, oil, bouillon granules, chervil, mustard and ground red pepper in jar with tight-fitting lid. Cover; shake well. Add to salad; toss to combine.

NUTRIENTS PER SERVING			
Calories	**54**	Cholesterol	**0mg**
Total fat	**2g**	Sodium	**79mg**
Protein	**3g**	Fiber	**2g**
Carbohydrate	**9g**		

GREENS AND BROCCOLI SALAD WITH PEPPY VINAIGRETTE

TABBOULEH

MAKES 8 SERVINGS

½ cup uncooked bulgur wheat
¾ cup boiling water
¼ teaspoon salt
5 teaspoons lemon juice
2 teaspoons olive oil
½ teaspoon dried basil leaves
¼ teaspoon black pepper
1 green onion, thinly sliced
½ cup chopped cucumber
½ cup chopped green bell pepper
½ cup chopped tomato
¼ cup chopped fresh parsley
2 teaspoons chopped mint (optional)

1. Rinse bulgur thoroughly in colander under cold water, picking out any debris. Drain well; transfer to medium heatproof bowl. Stir in boiling water and salt. Cover; let stand 30 minutes. Drain well.

2. Combine lemon juice, oil, basil and black pepper in small bowl. Pour over bulgur; mix well.

3. Layer bulgur, onion, cucumber, bell pepper and tomato in clear glass bowl; sprinkle with parsley and mint, if desired.

4. Refrigerate, covered, at least 2 hours to allow flavors to blend. Serve layered or toss before serving.

NUTRIENTS PER SERVING			
Calories	**49**	Cholesterol	**0mg**
Total fat	**1g**	Sodium	**71mg**
Protein	**1g**	Fiber	**3g**
Carbohydrate	**9g**		

SPICY ORIENTAL SHRIMP SALAD

MAKES 4 SERVINGS

1 head iceberg lettuce
½ cup fresh basil leaves
¼ cup rice wine vinegar
1 piece fresh ginger (2 inches), peeled
1 tablespoon reduced-sodium soy sauce
3 cloves garlic
1 teaspoon red pepper flakes
2 teaspoons dark sesame oil
28 large shrimp, peeled and deveined
1 to 2 limes, cut into wedges (optional)
Vinaigrette Dressing (recipe follows)

1. Core, rinse and thoroughly drain lettuce. Refrigerate in airtight container to crisp. Combine basil, vinegar, ginger, soy sauce, garlic, sesame oil and red pepper in blender or food processor fitted with metal blade. Blend to form rough paste, pulsing blender on and off, scraping sides as needed. Transfer paste to large mixing bowl. Add shrimp and stir until coated. Cover and refrigerate for 2 hours or overnight.

2. Preheat broiler. Broil shrimp in shallow pan, turning once, just until opaque, about 2 minutes each side. Shred lettuce; arrange on four plates. Top with cooked shrimp. Garnish with lime, if desired. Serve with Vinaigrette Dressing.

Vinaigrette Dressing: Whisk 3 tablespoons red wine vinegar with 1½ tablespoons olive oil in small bowl until blended.

NUTRIENTS PER SERVING			
Calories	**144**	Cholesterol	**75mg**
Total fat	**8g**	Sodium	**236mg**
Protein	**10g**	Fiber	**3g**
Carbohydrate	**7g**		

snack
solutions

HAM AND CHEESE "SUSHI" ROLLS

MAKES 8 SERVINGS

4 thin slices deli ham (about 4×4 inches)
1 package (8 ounces) cream cheese, softened
1 seedless cucumber, quartered lengthwise and cut into 4-inch lengths
4 thin slices (about 4×4 inches) American or Cheddar cheese, room temperature
1 red bell pepper, cut into thin 4-inch long strips

1. For ham sushi: Pat each ham slice with paper towel to remove excess moisture. Spread each ham slice to edges with 2 tablespoons cream cheese.

2. Pat 1 cucumber quarter with paper towel to remove excess moisture; place at edge of ham slice. Roll tightly. Seal by pressing gently. Roll in plastic wrap; refrigerate. Repeat with remaining three ham slices.

3. For cheese sushi: Spread each cheese slice to edges with 2 tablespoons cream cheese.

4. Place 2 strips red pepper even with one edge of one cheese slice. Roll tightly. Seal by pressing gently. Roll in plastic wrap; refrigerate. Repeat with remaining 3 cheese slices.

5. To serve: Remove plastic wrap from ham and cheese rolls. Cut each roll into 8 (½-inch-wide) pieces. Arrange on plate.

NUTRIENTS PER SERVING			
Calories	**145**	Cholesterol	**40mg**
Total fat	**13g**	Sodium	**263mg**
Protein	**5g**	Fiber	**<1g**
Carbohydrate	**3g**		

HAM AND CHEESE "SUSHI" ROLLS

WILD WEDGES

MAKES 4 SERVINGS

2 (8-inch) fat-free flour tortillas
Nonstick cooking spray
⅓ cup shredded reduced-fat Cheddar cheese
⅓ cup chopped cooked chicken or turkey
1 green onion, thinly sliced (about ¼ cup)
2 tablespoons mild, thick and chunky salsa

1. Heat large nonstick skillet over medium heat until hot.

2. Spray one side of one flour tortilla with cooking spray; place sprayed side down in skillet. Top with cheese, chicken, green onion and salsa. Place remaining tortilla over mixture; spray with cooking spray.

3. Cook 2 to 3 minutes per side or until golden brown and cheese is melted. Cut into 8 triangles.

Variation: For bean quesadillas, omit the chicken and spread ⅓ cup canned fat-free refried beans over one of the tortillas.

NUTRIENTS PER SERVING			
Calories	**76**	Cholesterol	**14mg**
Total fat	**2g**	Sodium	**282mg**
Protein	**7g**	Fiber	**4g**
Carbohydrate	**8g**		

WILD WEDGES

HERBED POTATO CHIPS

MAKES 6 SERVINGS

Nonstick olive oil cooking spray
2 medium red potatoes (about ½ pound), unpeeled
1 tablespoon olive oil
2 tablespoons minced fresh dill, thyme or rosemary *or* 2 teaspoons dried dill
weed, thyme or rosemary
¼ teaspoon garlic salt
⅛ teaspoon black pepper
1¼ cups fat-free sour cream

1. Preheat oven to 450°F. Spray large baking sheets with cooking spray; set aside.

2. Cut potatoes crosswise into very thin slices, about ¹⁄₁₆ inch thick. Pat dry with paper towels. Arrange potato slices in single layer on prepared baking sheets; coat potatoes with cooking spray.

3. Bake 10 minutes; turn slices over. Brush with oil. Combine dill, garlic salt and pepper in small bowl; sprinkle evenly onto potato slices. Continue baking 5 to 10 minutes or until potatoes are golden brown. Cool on baking sheets.

4. Serve with sour cream.

NUTRIENTS PER SERVING			
Calories	**76**	Cholesterol	**0mg**
Total fat	**2g**	Sodium	**113mg**
Protein	**6g**	Fiber	**<1g**
Carbohydrate	**9g**		

HERBED POTATO CHIPS

CONFETTI TUNA IN CELERY STICKS

MAKES 10 TO 12 SERVINGS

1 (3-ounce) pouch of STARKIST® Premium Albacore or Chunk Light Tuna
½ cup shredded red or green cabbage
½ cup shredded carrot
¼ cup shredded yellow squash or zucchini
3 tablespoons reduced-calorie cream cheese, softened
1 tablespoon plain low-fat yogurt
½ teaspoon dried basil, crushed
 Salt and pepper to taste
10 to 12 (4-inch) celery sticks, with leaves if desired

1. In a small bowl toss together tuna, cabbage, carrot and squash.

2. Stir in cream cheese, yogurt and basil. Add salt and pepper to taste.

3. With small spatula spread mixture evenly into celery sticks.

Prep Time: 20 minutes

NUTRIENTS PER SERVING			
Calories	32	Cholesterol	5mg
Total fat	1g	Sodium	90mg
Protein	3g	Fiber	1g
Carbohydrate	3g		

CONFETTI TUNA IN CELERY STICKS

SPICED SESAME WONTON CRISPS

MAKES 8 SERVINGS

20 (3-inch-square) wonton wrappers, cut in half
1 tablespoon water
2 teaspoons olive oil
½ teaspoon paprika
½ teaspoon ground cumin or chili powder
¼ teaspoon dry mustard
1 tablespoon sesame seeds

1. Preheat oven to 375°F. Coat 2 large nonstick baking sheets with nonstick cooking spray.

2. Cut each halved wonton wrapper into 2 strips; place in single layer on prepared baking sheets.

3. Combine water, oil, paprika, cumin and mustard in small bowl; mix well. Brush oil mixture evenly onto wonton strips; sprinkle evenly with sesame seeds.

4. Bake 6 to 8 minutes or until lightly browned. Remove to wire rack; cool completely. Transfer to serving plate.

NUTRIENTS PER SERVING			
Calories	**75**	Cholesterol	**3mg**
Total fat	**2g**	Sodium	**116mg**
Protein	**2g**	Fiber	**<1g**
Carbohydrate	**12g**		

SAVORY ZUCCHINI STIX

MAKES 4 SERVINGS

Nonstick olive oil cooking spray
3 tablespoons seasoned dry bread crumbs
2 tablespoons grated Parmesan cheese
1 egg white
1 teaspoon reduced-fat (2%) milk
2 small zucchini (about 4 ounces each), cut lengthwise into quarters
⅓ cup spaghetti sauce, warmed

1. Preheat oven to 400°F. Spray baking sheet with cooking spray; set aside.

2. Combine bread crumbs and Parmesan cheese in shallow dish. Combine egg white and milk in another shallow dish; beat with fork until well blended.

3. Dip each zucchini wedge first into crumb mixture, then into egg white mixture, letting excess drip back into dish. Roll again in crumb mixture to coat.

4. Place zucchini sticks on prepared baking sheet; coat well with cooking spray. Bake 15 to 18 minutes or until golden brown. Serve with spaghetti sauce.

NUTRIENTS PER SERVING			
Calories	**69**	Cholesterol	**6mg**
Total fat	**2g**	Sodium	**329mg**
Protein	**4g**	Fiber	**1g**
Carbohydrate	**9g**		

surprising
sweets

SPARKLING STRAWBERRY-LIME SHAKE

MAKES 2 SERVINGS

2 cups (10 ounces) frozen whole unsweetened strawberries
1¼ cups lime-flavored sparkling water, divided
¼ cup whipping cream or half-and-half
1 tablespoon sugar substitute
Lime wedges or slices

1. Place strawberries in blender container; allow to thaw 5 minutes before proceeding. Add 1 cup sparkling water, cream and sugar substitute. Cover; blend until smooth, scraping down sides of blender once or twice (mixture will be thick).

2. Gently stir in remaining sparkling water; pour into 2 glasses. Garnish with lime wedges.

Variation: For a tropical variation, add 1 teaspoon banana extract and/or ½ teaspoon coconut extract along with the cream. For a rum-flavored drink add ½ teaspoon rum extract. For quick shakes anytime, wash, hull and freeze whole strawberries in a tightly covered container.

NUTRIENTS PER SERVING			
Calories	**156**	Cholesterol	**41mg**
Total fat	**12g**	Sodium	**18mg**
Protein	**2g**	Fiber	**2g**
Carbohydrate	**15g**		

SPARKLING STRAWBERRY-LIME SHAKE

PINEAPPLE-GINGER BAVARIAN
MAKES 5 SERVINGS

1 can (8 ounces) crushed pineapple in juice, drained and liquid reserved
1 package (4-serving size) sugar-free orange gelatin
1 cup sugar-free ginger ale
1 cup plain nonfat yogurt
¾ teaspoon grated fresh ginger
½ cup whipping cream
1 packet sugar substitute
¼ teaspoon vanilla

1. Combine reserved pineapple juice with enough water to equal ½ cup liquid. Pour into small saucepan. Bring to a boil over high heat.

2. Place gelatin in medium bowl. Add pineapple juice mixture; stir until gelatin is completely dissolved. Add ginger ale and half of crushed pineapple; stir until well blended. Add yogurt; whisk until well blended. Pour into 5 individual ramekins. Cover each ramekin with plastic wrap; refrigerate until firm.

3. Meanwhile, combine remaining half of crushed pineapple with ginger in small bowl. Cover with plastic wrap; refrigerate.

4. Just before serving, beat cream in small deep bowl on high speed of electric mixer until soft peaks form. Add sugar substitute and vanilla; beat until stiff peaks form.

5. To serve, top bavarian with 1 tablespoon whipped topping and 1 tablespoon pineapple mixture.

NUTRIENTS PER SERVI1MG			
Calories	**76**	Cholesterol	**1mg**
Total fat	**1g**	Sodium	**102mg**
Protein	**4g**	Fiber	**<1g**
Carbohydrate	**12g**		

PINEAPPLE-GINGER BAVARIANS

CHOCOLATE PEANUT BUTTER ICE CREAM SANDWICHES

MAKES 4 SERVINGS

2 tablespoons creamy peanut butter
8 chocolate wafer cookies
⅔ cup no-sugar-added vanilla ice cream, softened

1. Spread peanut butter over flat sides of all cookies

2. Spoon ice cream over peanut butter on 4 cookies. Top with remaining 4 cookies, peanut butter sides down. Press down lightly to force ice cream to edges of sandwich.

3. Wrap each sandwich in foil; seal tightly. Freeze at least 2 hours or up to 5 days.

NUTRIENTS PER SERVING			
Calories	**129**	Cholesterol	**4mg**
Total fat	**7g**	Sodium	**124mg**
Protein	**4g**	Fiber	**1g**
Carbohydrate	**15g**		

WHITE CHOCOLATE PUDDING PARFAITS

MAKES 4 SERVINGS

1 package (4-serving size) sugar-free instant white chocolate pudding mix
2 cups (low-fat) 2% milk
¾ cup whipping cream
1½ cups fresh raspberries or sliced strawberries
2 tablespoons chopped roasted shelled pistachio nuts or chopped toasted macadamia nuts

1. Add pudding mix to milk; beat with wire whisk or electric mixer 2 minutes. Refrigerate 5 minutes or until thickened. Beat whipping cream in small deep bowl with electric mixer at high speed until stiff peaks form. Fold whipped cream into pudding.

2. In each of 4 parfait or wine glasses, layer ¼ cup pudding and 2 tablespoons raspberries. Repeat layers. Spoon remaining pudding over berries. Serve immediately or cover and chill up to 6 hours before serving. Just before serving, sprinkle with nuts.

NUTRIENTS PER SERVING			
Calories	**284**	Cholesterol	**71mg**
Total fat	**21g**	Sodium	**291mg**
Protein	**7g**	Fiber	**4g**
Carbohydrate	**19g**		

CHOCOLATE PEANUT BUTTER ICE CREAM SANDWICHES

ANGEL CAKE WITH ALMOND BUTTER SAUCE
MAKES 16 SERVINGS

1 prepared angel food cake (14 ounces)
8 ounces sliced almonds
2 cups (4 sticks) butter
14 packages sugar substitute
1 teaspoon ground cinnamon
½ teaspoon ground nutmeg

1. Preheat oven to 325°F.

2. Cut cake into 16 slices with serrated knife. Arrange cake slices accordion-fashion on ovenproof serving plate. Cover with foil; bake 10 minutes or until heated through.

3. Meanwhile, place 12-inch nonstick skillet over medium-high heat until hot. Add almonds; cook and stir 4 minutes or until lightly browned. Remove from pan; set aside.

4. Heat butter in same skillet over medium heat until bubbly. Remove from heat; stir in sugar substitute, cinnamon and nutmeg.

5. Arrange warm cake on serving platter; sprinkle with almonds evenly. Spoon butter mixture over cake.

NUTRIENTS PER SERVING			
Calories	**358**	Cholesterol	**62mg**
Total fat	**30g**	Sodium	**420mg**
Protein	**5g**	Fiber	**2g**
Carbohydrate	**18g**		

ANGEL CAKE WITH ALMOND BUTTER SAUCE

CHOCOLATE-ALMOND MERINGUE PUFFS

MAKES 15 SERVINGS

2 tablespoons granulated sugar
3 packages sugar substitute
1½ teaspoons unsweetened cocoa powder
2 egg whites, room temperature
½ teaspoon vanilla
¼ teaspoon cream of tartar
¼ teaspoon almond extract
⅛ teaspoon salt
1½ ounces sliced almonds
3 tablespoons sugar-free seedless raspberry fruit spread

1. Preheat oven to 275°F. Combine granulated sugar, sugar substitute and cocoa powder in small bowl; set aside.

2. Beat egg whites in small bowl on high speed of electric mixer until foamy. Add vanilla, cream of tartar, almond extract and salt; beat until soft peaks form. Add sugar mixture, 1 tablespoon at a time, beating until stiff peaks form.

3. Line baking sheet with foil. Spoon 15 equal mounds of egg white mixture onto foil. Sprinkle with almonds.

4. Bake 1 hour. Turn oven off but do not open oven door. Leave puffs in oven 2 hours longer or until completely dry. Remove from oven; cool completely.

5. Stir fruit spread and spoon about ½ teaspoon onto each meringue just before serving.

Tip: Puffs are best if eaten the same day they're made. If necessary, store in airtight container, adding fruit topping at time of serving.

NUTRIENTS PER SERVING			
Calories	**34**	Cholesterol	**0mg**
Total fat	**1g**	Sodium	**27mg**
Protein	**1g**	Fiber	**<1g**
Carbohydrate	**4g**		

CHOCOLATE-ALMOND MERINGUE PUFFS

STRAWBERRY-TOPPED CHEESECAKE CUPS

MAKES 8 SERVINGS

　1 cup sliced strawberries
10 packages sugar substitute, divided
　1 teaspoon vanilla, divided
½ teaspoon grated orange peel
¼ teaspoon grated fresh ginger
　1 package (8 ounces) cream cheese, softened
½ cup sour cream
　2 tablespoons granulated sugar
16 vanilla wafers, crushed

1. Combine strawberries, 1 package sugar substitute, ¼ teaspoon vanilla, orange peel and grated ginger in medium bowl; toss gently. Let stand 20 minutes to allow flavors to blend.

2. Meanwhile, combine cream cheese, sour cream, remaining 9 packets sugar substitute and granulated sugar in medium mixing bowl. Add remaining ¾ teaspoon vanilla; beat 30 seconds on low speed of electric mixer. Increase to medium speed; beat 30 seconds or until smooth.

3. Spoon cream cheese mixture into 8 individual ¼-cup ramekins. Top each with about 2 tablespoons vanilla wafer crumbs and about 2 tablespoons strawberry mixture.

NUTRIENTS PER SERVING			
Calories	**205**	Cholesterol	**36mg**
Total fat	**15g**	Sodium	**127mg**
Protein	**3g**	Fiber	**<1g**
Carbohydrate	**15g**		

STRAWBERRY-TOPPED CHEESECAKE CUPS

CHOCOLATE CHEESECAKE

MAKES 10 SERVINGS

2 packages (8 ounces each) cream cheese, softened
2 eggs
⅓ cup plus 2 teaspoons granular sugar substitute,* divided
2 tablespoons honey
3 teaspoons vanilla, divided
2 level tablespoons unsweetened cocoa
1 cup heavy whipping cream

*Choose a sugar substitute that measures like sugar, such as Splenda® or Equal® Spoonful.

1. Preheat oven to 350°F. Spray 8-inch round cake pan with nonstick cooking spray. Cut 8-inch parchment paper or wax paper circle to fit bottom of pan. Place paper in pan; spray lightly with cooking spray.

2. Beat cream cheese, eggs, ⅓ cup sugar substitute, honey and 2 teaspoons vanilla in large bowl or electric mixer at medium speed 2 to 3 minutes just until well blended. With mixer running on low speed, beat in cocoa until well blended. *Do not overbeat.*

3. Pour batter into prepared pan. Bake 35 to 40 minutes until center is set. Cool 10 minutes on wire rack; run thin spatula around edge of cheesecake to loosen. Cool completely.

4. Invert cheesecake onto plate. Remove parchment paper. Place serving plate over cake; invert cake top side up. Cover loosely with plastic wrap. Refrigerate at least 4 hours or overnight.

5. Beat cream, remaining 2 teaspoons sugar substitute and 1 teaspoon vanilla in small deep bowl at high speed of electric mixer until stiff peaks form. Serve with cheesecake.

NUTRIENTS PER SERVING			
Calories	**296**	Cholesterol	**125mg**
Total fat	**27g**	Sodium	**158mg**
Protein	**6g**	Fiber	**<1g**
Carbohydrate	**7g**		

CHOCOLATE CHEESECAKE

PEANUT BUTTER CHOCOLATE BARS

MAKES 48 SERVINGS

½ cup (1 stick) butter or margarine, softened
1 cup EQUAL® SPOONFUL*
⅓ cup firmly packed brown sugar
½ cup 2% milk
½ cup creamy peanut butter
1 egg
1 teaspoon vanilla
1 cup all-purpose flour
1 cup quick oats, uncooked
½ teaspoon baking soda
¼ teaspoon salt
¾ cup mini semi-sweet chocolate chips

*May substitute 24 packets Equal® sweetener.

• Beat butter, Equal® and brown sugar until well combined. Stir in milk, peanut butter, egg and vanilla until blended. Gradually mix in combined flour, oats, baking soda and salt until blended. Stir in chocolate chips.

• Spread mixture evenly in 13×9-inch baking pan generously coated with nonstick cooking spray. Bake in preheated 350°F oven 20 to 22 minutes. Cool completely in pan on wire rack. Cut into squares; store in airtight container at room temperature.

NUTRIENTS PER SERVING			
Calories	75	Cholesterol	10mg
Total fat	5g	Sodium	60mg
Protein	1g	Fiber	1g
Carbohydrate	8g		

INDEX

ACKNOWLEDGMENTS

The publisher would like to thank the companies and organizations listed below for the use of their recipes and photographs in this publication.

Butterball® Turkey

Egg Beaters®

Equal® sweetener

Hershey Foods Corporation

Splenda® is a registered trademark of McNeil Nutritionals

StarKist® Seafood Company